MW00471509

Cast the First Stone
by Michael Burkhalter

Published by Volo Press Books, LLC
Cover Design by Volo Press Books, LLC
Cover Illustration by Landon Green
Editing and Formatting by Volo Press Books, LLC
Cast the First Stone
Library of Congress Control Number: 2019904985
ISBN: 978-1-7337377-1-5

10 9 8 7 6 5 4 3 2 1
1. Religion – Christian Living – Spiritual Growth
2. Self-help – Spiritual

First Edition

Printed in the United States of America

Table of Contents

Foreword

I have heard that there are two reasons why people don't go to church. Either they don't know a Christian or, even worse, they *do* know a Christian. As Christians we have the opportunity and obligation to represent Christ in every facet of our lives. When we claim to know a loving God and then live a life that doesn't reflect that love, we send a message— the *wrong* message.

Have you ever wondered why the traditional Christian religious community in America seems to be something so many people have an issue with? I believe this is because we, as God's children, have a lot of trouble letting go of all our worldly desires. Sometimes we would rather incorporate Jesus into our lives because we fear Hell rather than because we truly love God. Jesus said in **Mark 8:34-35**(NKJV), "Whoever desires to come after Me, let him deny himself, and take up his cross, and follow me. For whoever desires to save his life will lose it, but whoever loses his life for my sake and the gospel's will save it."

In Michael's book, he lays out some of the sins that are holding the church back from manifesting the love of God. As followers of Christ we need to be representing Him to the world around us, and we cannot do this the way God intended when we are self-righteous. I think Michael did an amazing job of outlining the reasons so many believers hang on to their self-righteousness. This book has been a help to me by showing me that I need to stop comparing myself to other people to make myself feel better about my right standing with God. I didn't consider myself a self-righteous person. I would have called myself humble, but in many aspects of my life I was looking for the approval of people in life rather than God Himself. Therefore, I urge all you brothers and sisters in

Christ to look at your own lives with humility. Whether you are a Bible scholar or a brand-new believer, I encourage you to look deep into your conscience and consider what is truly motivating you and what you are doing with the opportunity Christ has given you to represent His Kingdom.

—Jesse Haack
Dear friend and student of Michael Burkhalter

Introduction

Throughout my experiences with individuals, families, and couples, I have seen a major problem with judgement, criticism, ostracism, and ridicule, as if we are not all God's creation.

I wrote this book in response to seeing this pattern among people who call themselves "Christians." I'm not here to hypocritically judge and criticize any of my fellow human beings for the shortcomings you (and I!) possess. My goal is to point out common mistakes that I have seen people make as they attempt to live the word of God so that you can work toward not taking those same missteps.

When it comes to various aspects of our current daily life, I think we all can strive to treat people a little bit better than we did the day before. I hope you will read each chapter with your Bible at hand. I will be noting passages from the New King James version and I will repeatedly encourage you to read scriptures that are pertinent to the content of each chapter and the overall message of this book. I have put cited verses in **bold** so that they're easy to see and refer to as needed.

One thing you'll notice about this book is that it is full of questions. And they aren't just there for show. I want you to consider how well you are following the teachings of Christ and the word of God in your daily life. I want you to take personal inventory of your spiritual health and will prompt you to do so page after page, chapter after chapter. If done with an honest mind and an open heart, this ongoing spiritual self-assessment is sure to be thoroughly uncomfortable. However, I can guarantee you it will be worth it to make sure you are serving God as best you can every day of your life that He blesses you with.

At the end of each chapter, I offer you reflective questions to help you gain perspective on who you are as a worshipper of God. Please take your time reviewing these questions and be authentic in your responses. You may run up against difficult truths about yourself, your congregation, and your faith, but I want you to use those newfound truths to create a better future for yourself as a Christian.

The namesake of this book, and the crux of its message, lies in the scenario in which Jesus was confronted with a woman who was caught red-handed in the act of committing adultery. The Pharisees wanted Jesus to agree that this woman should be stoned to death, as Moses had proclaimed an adulterer like her should be.

Take a few moments to read the full story in **John 8** and think about who best represents **you** in this situation: the Pharisees, the onlookers, the woman, or Jesus.

"So, when they continued asking Him, He raised Himself up and said to them, "He who is without sin among you, let him throw a stone at her first.""

—John 8:7

Chapter 1
Christian in Name Only

I'm going to outline a lot of things that I see as mistakes well-meaning Christians are making when it comes to worshipping God in their daily lives. However, I think that the core idea behind all the mistakes lies in the three commandments that sum up what, in my view, a Christian is really supposed to be.

We've all been taught the Ten Commandments in Sunday school. I want to let you know right now that there were 613 commandments given in the Bible, referred to as the "Mosaic Laws". I could spend pages upon pages listing and explaining all 613 of these laws, but I'll let you read those for yourself in the first five books of the Old Testament.

However, I will devote a few paragraphs to letting you know that most Christians follow virtually none of those laws today, breaking them on a weekly or daily basis. For example, you're not supposed to overeat. Haven't you grabbed an extra cookie or ordered one more side of macaroni and cheese after you've finished your meal? As a nation, don't we have a serious problem with obesity?

According to the Mosaic Laws, we're also supposed to stand in the presence of our elders. Do you consistently stand for people who are older than you, simply because they walked into the room? Is it physically possible for you to do so if you spend time around your elders on a regular basis (working in a retirement home, for example)?

Do you own any clothing that's made from two different kinds of materials (mixing fabrics)? That's against the law. How long could you go wearing only the things in your closet that are made from 100% of a single fabric?

According to the Mosaic Laws of the Bible, you are not supposed to eat fat. This would mean that virtually any meat, nuts, dairy, and even some fruits and vegetable oils would need to be eliminated from your diet. Could you stand to be on a no-fat diet for the rest of your life?

And the last time your child misbehaved (acted out, talked back, didn't do their homework, etc.), you were supposed to take them to the elders in your neighborhood and have them stoned to death. If you allowed your misbehaving child to live, you broke yet another law from the Bible.

As important as it is to understand and accept that you break these laws every day, it's also helpful for you to understand that *none* of them have anything to do with you if you are not part of one of the twelve tribes of Israel. Jesus told us that He was the fulfillment of all those laws and that we were no longer bound by them. Yet, we still try to push some (not all, for some reason) of those laws onto other people (I'll go into more detail on this in the third chapter). I encourage you to take a different approach to Christianity and simply try to obey the three commandments that Jesus gave. Each of the following chapters will discuss these commandments in detail, with the fifth chapter offering options to help you more closely follow what Jesus has asked us to do in the name of His Father.

The Three Commandments

1. Love your Lord your God with all your heart and mind.
2. Love your neighbor as yourself.
3. Go and make disciples.

Those seem easy enough, don't they? So why is it we as Christians cannot do these three simple things we were asked to do by The Savior? My answer: Because we do not want to. We do not want it to be that easy. As Christians we tend to think everything must be complicated and nothing can be simple. When the truth is it *really is* that simple. You might be thinking: *It took 613 laws, a high priest, and animal sacrifices to get us to the Messiah. How in the world could being a devoted Christian be boiled down to those three commandments?*

Jesus was the sacrifice for all of us and all He asked us to do in return were these basic things. In the following chapters, we'll walk through each one and focus on how we can be better Christians by following what Jesus told us to do, not what *we* want to do!

Chapter Summary

There were over 600 original commandments. Did you know
that already? How does it feel to learn this or to hear it again?

_____

_____

_____

_____

_____

_____

_____

_____

_____

When Jesus ascended into Heaven, He reduced those 613
commandments down to just three. Why do you think He did
that for us?

_____

_____

_____

Do you already follow any of the three commandments on a
consistent basis? Which ones could you do better with?

_____

_____

_____

_____

_____

_____

_____

_____

_____

If you adhered to these three principles, how do you think your life could change (your relationships, your work, your self-esteem, etc.)?

_____

_____

_____

_____

_____

Chapter 2
Loving God

Love your God with all your heart and mind.

How are you doing with this one? Do you still praise God even when you are going through a storm? Do you get mad at God for not answering a prayer? Did you ever think that, as His children, He has our best interests in mind? Maybe that job promotion would have taken too much time away from your family. Maybe He knows you won't help the needy if you do get those lottery winnings you've been begging for.

We get so mad at God for not doing what we want we're like children throwing a temper tantrum when we don't get a new toy. As parents, we think we know what's best for our children and do everything in our power to make sure they have what they need. So why do you not trust our heavenly father to have your best interests in mind? Do you not think He is capable? Or do you just like to throw a tantrum? Turn on the evening news tonight. I think you will see humanity has been throwing a tantrum for a very long time now!

Loving God is about worshipping and obeying God. If you're wondering how best to do this, it is by obeying the next two commandments outlined in the following chapters. When you love your neighbor, you show respect for one of God's creations. And when you go out into the world in order to make disciples, you show love for God and His will by showing other's the light that is God and our savior Jesus Christ.

Again: This is not what I am seeing with most Christians! I see plenty of selfishness, judgment, greed, and criticism that shouldn't be what Christians show to the world.

I believe that this is a big part of the reason that so many people turn away from Christianity and God. Not because of the principles of Christianity (who doesn't want peace and love on Earth?), but because of the *people* non-believers encounter when they attempt to interact with a church or a so-called Christian.

This is a topic very near to my heart. I have personally witnessed this "false advertisement" destroy a non-believer's openness to accept the gift of salvation offered by our Lord Jesus Christ.

John's Story

I was raised by a Christian man and woman who made sure I not only was at church when I should be but also understood what the true meaning of grace was and that it was bestowed upon us, therefore we should bestow it upon others. For these teachings from them I am eternally thankful.

As a boy, I had a friend, John, who was raised by outspoken Atheists. As a matter of fact, his parents did not like me as a friend choice for that very reason. We remained friends despite our different upbringings and for years I tried to get him to come to church with my family and me. Of course. he always declined, mostly out of fear of what his own parents would do if he said 'yes'.

After years of friendship, John's mother was tragically taken in an automobile accident. As I tried to comfort my friend, his father asked me very politely to leave his son alone, which I did since I had been raised to respect my elders.

After the funeral, John came to me and said, "All these years you wanted me to go to church and I never understood why. Now that the realization of my mother being gone forever has set in, I would like to go at least hear about this eternal life thing you keep talking about."

I could not have been happier! But I wanted to be careful and not overwhelm with too much too fast. So, I decided that, instead of throwing him into the fire of an actual worship service, I would ease him into the kiddie pool of a youth event being held by one of the local churches in our town. As the day of the event drew nearer, I could barely contain my excitement. All those years of putting in the effort to get John into church were finally paying off. We met up as agreed and walked inside the building.

Just as we had taken a seat inside the church, a "Deacon" of the church came up to us.

"Son," he said, looking at John, "I'm afraid I'm gonna have to ask you to leave."

I was both surprised and confused until I saw where the man was looking—right at John's long hair, well-groomed as it was. Not unruly or unkempt, brightly colored or outrageously styled, lice-ridden or sprinkled with dandruff, simply a few inches longer than some young men our age kept their hair.

The man said, "We don't believe men should look like that and you are not welcome here."

John was obviously offended. But he, too, had been raised to respect his elders, so he just got up and walked out without another word. I was devastated and hurt. I got up to follow him, but the man stopped me.

"Hey now, son, *you're* welcome to stay!"

Now anger started to rise inside me, and I turned to him and said, "Not only will I not stay another second in what you call a "church," but I will pray for you to understand what you have just done!" I spun around and walked out after John.

As you may imagine, John was very upset. When he finally spoke, his words made me feel even more disappointed.

"*This* is what you were raving about? This is the Jesus you follow? I came to hear about hope and acceptance and instead I got judgement and ridicule because I don't look the way *they* think I should look!"

I was at a loss for words. As upset as he was, he was right. It took me fifteen years of witnessing to a non-believer to get him inside a church, and all of fifteen seconds for a "Christian" to destroy his hope.

John had come looking for comfort in God's love and got the judgment of the church.

How would you feel if Jesus treated you the way that church treated John? Would you want Jesus to judge you based on your clothes, car, jewelry, or hair style? Last I looked, Jesus always had to correct the church, and consistently hung out with what the church saw as irredeemable trash. Have we really become the Pharisees? Have we forgotten that Jesus said, "I came for everyone" and *lived* that way? It seems all we do as a church anymore is pass judgment. What happened to accepting the lost with love and grace? Jesus did it for you, even if you are a front-pew, judgmental Christian.

Only by God's grace and will, a few years after that incident, John came to me and said he would like to try church one more time. He said he may have jumped to a conclusion based on the loss he had just experienced. I refused to take him back to church because I couldn't stand the thought of someone else treating John like they had before. Instead, I suggested we go to a homeless shelter and work for a night so he could truly see what following Jesus was about. He laughed and said he didn't understand, but he agreed to go anyway.

After an hour or so of us being there, a very old Black man we all knew as "Preacher Man" got up and offered to bless the meal. In the prayer he didn't ask for money or a home or any kind of earthly possessions or selfish desires. He simply asked for God to bless the food they were given and then he said something that moved the mountain that blocked the door to John's heart.

"God, I have nothing on the Earth but a lot of treasure in Heaven. Can you please send some down for me to give away?"

Almost immediately after that prayer, Preacher Man looked up and made eye contact with John. He walked up to John and started a conversation about John's hair and how nice it looked. After about an hour of food and conversation, my Atheist friend who had been shunned by the church finally gave his life to God. John experienced the miracle and I got to see it.

That was the first time that I truly understood that it wasn't the inside of your church that mattered, it was what was in your heart. A church asked my friend to leave because of his hair, a homeless man lead him to God because of his hair. Now who showed the love of God: the church or the homeless man?

Every day I hear stupid ideas coming out of so-called Christians' mouths. I see churches attacking churches because of the dogma of humans attacking humans over looks, money, or sexuality. We have a certain set of traditions in the church that have nothing to do with worshipping God, or living in His word, but everything to do with worshipping the traditions themselves because "that's the way we've always done it." So many Christians fall into a trap of doing things that are not part of the Christian faith (such as asking a young boy to leave an event because of the length of his hair) just because that's what they've been shown or how they've been raised. But every now and then God sends us someone like Preacher Man to show that love is what's important, not dogma or tradition.

I encourage you as someone who wants to be a better Christian to stop just "playing church" (showing up to be seen or to gossip and not to worship) and *love* like Preacher Man did. Like Jesus tells us all to do.

My friend John went on to become a pastor. He started a church for the homeless. His family is doing well, and he was even able to eventually lead his dad to the Lord. Not because of a judgmental church that didn't like his hair, but because of a homeless man who did.

But this is only one aspect of a general tendency in the Christian community to not show the love of God to ourselves or in our interactions with others. There are too many to list here, but I'll highlight some just to give you an idea of what I mean.

Loving God Shows the Way

How can a professed Christian say they want to move people to Christ but won't allow certain people in their church? Christ encouraged us love our neighbors and even our enemies. In following this principle, we honor God and show others who don't believe that they should follow God and *why* they should follow God. Behaving in the ways that Jesus commanded can attract people to our faith. And when you make people *want* to be part of Christianity—because you show them how loving we are, not because you point out their sins or beat them over the head with scripture—they're more likely to develop a strong faith and follow God for the rest of their lives.

Christ did not side with the Pharisees. He regularly reprimanded them and pointed out how they often behaved worse than the people they were condemning. I recommend leaving the responsibility for judging other people in God's hands, where it belongs. As His worshipper, just focus on showing his love to those around you.

Laws Not Meant for You

The 613 Mosaic Laws were meant for the Hebrews. If you're not Jewish, they did not, and do not, apply to you. Jesus also made it very clear that He was the fulfillment of those laws through His crucifixion, death, and resurrection. Luckily, instead of having to remember and be bound to obey 613 laws, you now just need to concern yourself with three commandments.

Grasping Grace

God's grace is the only reason any of us are where we are in life—the only reason we exist. Regardless of the various sins that we commit on a weekly, daily, or even hourly basis, God decides to show us love and compassion. Yet, even though we experience this daily example of grace firsthand, when someone does or says or believes something we don't agree with, we're quick to mock them, avoid them, shame them, and judge them. We should be passing along the gift of grace that God has given us so that we can draw more people toward following Christian teachings instead of scaring them away with our criticism and self-righteous attitudes. The Bible tells us that no sin is greater than any other. So, unless you have committed no sins at all (just a hint: this is never the case so long as you are human), you have no right to think less of someone else simply because their sin is *different* from your sin.

The Christian favorite "Amazing Grace" opens with the lyrics, "Amazing grace how sweet the sound that saved a wretch like me." How is your grace? Are you giving it as freely as it is being given to you?

Tradition vs Truth

South Carolina is steeped in traditions, like many portions of the southern United States. Unfortunately, the church has adopted a lot of things that are traditions and not biblical truths. For example, there is a tradition of wearing one's finest clothing on Sundays. I am sure you have heard everything on this topic from "come as you are" to "dress modestly" to "always wear your Sunday best".

I think the idea that someone must dress in their best clothing to attend church is a silly one. Not only does your clothing have nothing to do with whether or not, or how much, you can worship God at church, but putting any sort of emphasis on the importance of how you dress actually flies in the face of what scripture says. You'll find that **James 2: 1 – 4** states: "My brethren, do no hold the faith of our Lord Jesus Christ, the Lord of glory, with partiality. For if there should come into your assembly a man with gold rings, in fine apparel, and there should also come in a poor man in filthy clothes, and you pay attention to the one wearing the fine clothes and say to him, "You sit here in a good place," and say to the poor man, "You stand there," or, "Sit here at my footstool," have you not shown partiality among yourselves, and become judges with evil thoughts?"

For those who are familiar with the Bible, you may think that **Timothy 2: 9 – 10** tells us to dress modestly, but that section is often taken out of context. These verses are about how we approach God, not how we dress for church worship. Ideas and traditions like this can only serve as a barrier between Christianity and the people who might benefit from it the most. Why would anyone want to attend a service or interact with people who they assume are going to judge them about what they're wearing?

Dress as you feel comfortable. For any believer, the Holy Spirit should make you feel comfortable if modesty is an issue. Remember that Adam and Eve were brought into the world naked and remained that way *until* the serpent got involved. Then clothing became a priority for humans. Do you really think that, as long as you come to Him with an open heart, He cares what you have on?

Beyond the tradition of "dressing up" for services on Sunday, I have been in churches that only allow traditional gospel hymns. I have also attended churches that allow modern worship music to be played. Unfortunately, humans tend to allow musical styles to dictate an acceptance or rejection of a song. Again, our ideas—not God's ideas—have gotten in the way. The Bible doesn't say much about this topic. One of the closest biblical descriptions we have is in **Ephesians 5:19-21**: "address one another in psalms and hymns and spiritual songs, singing and making melody to the Lord with your heart, giving thanks always and for everything to the Father, in the name of our lord Jesus Christ, submitting to one another out of reverence for Christ." That sounds like a call for unity to me, not dissention. We all need to realize that our musical preferences are just that—a preference. Our preferences are not biblical at all, but traditional. The Bible tells us to make a joyful noise to the Lord. Not make only sounds and music that you like to hear! If your church spends their energy on whether or not traditional or modern worship music will be played in the sanctuary, maybe you should find one that is more concerned about bringing people to Christ and not what music is played on Sunday morning.

In the next chapter, we'll go into more detail about the different ways we can (but often don't!) love our neighbors like ourselves.

"Tradition becomes our security, and when the mind is secure it is in decay."

—Jiddu Krishnamurti

Chapter Summary

We often get angry at God for not doing our will instead of trying to do His will. Is there something you've been praying to get for a long time? Can you think of a few reasons why God might not be answering that prayer?

_____

_____

_____

_____

_____

Do you find yourself judging people who don't act, look, worship, or talk like you? Do you label them as boring, unintelligent, incompetent, weird, lazy, or scary? Do you think Jesus would judge or criticize those people if He were meeting them face to face?

_____

_____

_____

_____

_____

_____

_____

_____

_____

Why do you make the judgements you make about people?
What does your judgement of others say about you as a
person?

_____

_____

_____

_____

_____

_____

_____

_____

_____

_____

Between John (an Atheist seeking God), the deacon (a
Christian banning someone from the church based on how
they look), and me (someone trying to help a non-believer
understand God's love), who do you think you most resemble
in your daily life? Are you regularly seeking God out and
bringing others to Him, or are you acting as a 'bouncer' for the
church to keep the "riff raff" out?

_____

_____

_____

_____

_____

_____

_____

_____

_____

Are you worshipping God and His word or man-made traditions in your church life? Give examples.

_____

_____

_____

_____

_____

What are some traditions you see in the church that don't have anything to do with Biblical law? Does keeping with these man-made traditions ever keep people out of your congregation or make newcomers feel unwelcome? What can you do to help fix that in your church?

_____

_____

_____

_____

_____

_____

_____

_____

_____

Chapter 3
Loving Neighbors

Love your neighbor as yourself.

Ouch! Now here is one that very few of us understand, much less do. So why is this so hard? Shouldn't it be simple to love your fellow man? Sure. Or, it *could* be. But here comes that "Christian" in us. We would rather judge people than love them. Although we are told repeatedly not to do that by Jesus. If we all followed this one commandment, I would have virtually no material for this book.

As I outline in the last chapter, following this commandment often takes minimal effort and costs us nothing but our time and willingness. Yet very few of us accomplish the things we could do to show love to our neighbor (greeting them warmly when we see them, helping them when they're in need, listening when something is on their mind, etc.) on a regular basis, and most of us don't do them at all. Ask yourself how we can expect the kingdom of God to grow if we don't even know something as simple as our neighbor's name?

We don't want to reach out and love others. We barely even seem to want to physically interact with other human beings on a consistent basis. In this chapter, I'll highlight a few (though not nearly all) of the topics that divide us as Christians and cause us to try to represent and further our own personal agendas rather than those of God. These are topics that push us to *not* love our neighbors, even though the people we shun, avoid, or blatantly disrespect need and deserve God's love, too.

Homophobia

Let's start with the most common form of fear and hatred I see in the average church today. 'Homophobia' means 'a fear of homosexual people'. So why does the church fear these people? What's so special about homosexuality versus murder, adultery, gluttony, and the rest?

The book that just about any churchgoer will have thrown at them when the topic of homosexuality arises in conversation or study is Leviticus. Namely, **Leviticus 20:13** that states: "If a man lies with a male as he lies with a woman, both of them have committed an abomination. They shall surely be put to death. Their blood *shall be* upon them."

What an easy and convenient verse to hide behind. Most Christians have no idea what the book of Leviticus is and, more to the point, who it was meant for. But they certainly have no problem quoting this verse when addressing homosexuality.

As I've stated previously, this is one of the laws meant for a group of people that does not include Christians, and for a time that has long passed. These old laws aren't meant to have any bearing on our lives today, so quoting this piece of scripture is like reciting a curfew given to you by your parents when you were twelve years old. You're not twelve anymore and your relationship with your parents (in theory) has changed drastically since you were a pre-teen. So, what is the point of bringing up your curfew (or any other rule) from that outdated, irrelevant situation? Quoting verses from Leviticus works the same way. Leviticus is a book of laws given to Moses to govern the *Hebrew* people, not everyone.

If you believe that the Hebrew rule about homosexuality should be applied to homosexuals, then you should also be following all of those same laws yourself (no fat, no mixed fabrics, no living disobedient children, etc.). Sexual orientation doesn't have anything to do with someone doing the right thing or being a good person. But, based on some of the sermons I have been to, that is exactly what a lot of people think.

In the paragraphs below, I am going to give you some examples of several well-known people (you've seen them all on television and in movies, read about them in textbooks, and heard them on the radio) without giving you their names. Guess who they are as you read about the things each one has done.

Subject A

Used his God given talent to rise to fame in the music industry in the late eighties. He donated all the sales of one of the songs he wrote to kids fighting cancer. On one evening, he was watching a game show and learned that one of the contestants went on the game show to try and win money for his wife's in vitro fertilization treatment. He was so moved by the husband, he found out the contestant's name and called the next day to give them the money to pay for the treatment in its entirety. He also once paid for an entire year of nursing school for a waitress he had met who was working and raising kids alone so she could become a nurse and better her and her kids' lives.

Do you know this person?

Subject B

One of the most recognizable faces in television. After achieving fame, she has donated millions of dollars to charity, helped rebuild a school in Detroit, and almost on a daily basis looks for someone that is doing good for the community and donates money to their cause.

Who could this be?

Subject C

A man who started as a powerful pastor and ultimately used his power to grow his congregation into a massive church. He had plenty of outreach programs and took in those people other churches refused to allow in their doors.

Sound familiar?

Subject D

This man started as a man of faith and became a powerful leader. He preached tolerance of all and love of all. His congregation grew to such a size that even the government took notice. He always preached what he felt was true from the Bible and always looked out for his flock.

Guess who!

Were you able to recognize any of these famous people? Take a moment to think about which of these four people your church would welcome into your congregation.

All of them? The ones with money? The ones who gathered their own flock of Christians? They all seem to be doing God's work. Take a look at the identities of these subjects:

Subject A:
George Michael—singer, songwriter, openly gay.

Subject B:
Ellen DeGeneres—actress, talk show host, openly gay.

Subject C:
Jim Jones—pastor, cult leader, murderer.

Subject D:
David Koresh—pastor, cult leader, murderer.

So how did you do with those four? Would your church be more prone to allow the first two in or the second two without knowing anything but their works? Did the fact that the last two were pastors do anything to influence your thinking?

A lot of people can "be" the right thing (i.e.: pastor, teacher, choir member, etc.) and still do terrible things. Just as someone can be gay and do wonderful, compassionate, loving things for their fellow man (as Jesus told us to do) regardless of their religious affiliation, or lack thereof.

To be clear: I do not agree with the homosexual lifestyle at all. All I know is, the God I follow told me not to judge, but to love. God has also relayed the message that their sin is no different from my sin. And that if you confess and ask to be saved, you will be. No matter what you look like, where you come from, or who you sleep with.

Racism

Racism is a very sensitive subject in my neck of the woods, South Carolina. And while there are a lot of different opinions and attitudes about race and racism politically and socially, in this book I want to focus on racism biblically.

What does the Bible say about racism? Today, we consider there to be many races such as Black, White, Indian, or Asian. But there is only one actual race—human.

All of us are made in the image of God. You can find that in the very first book of the Bible (**Genesis 1:26-27**). In the most well-known verse in the Bible, **John 3:16**, the word 'world' means 'the human race.' It does not say "for He so loved the White guy" or "for He so loved the Jews" but "for He so loved the world." That's everybody, not just one nation, race, or ethnicity.

In the Old Testament, God meant for the Jew to minister to the gentile. But that ugly thing called human nature got in the way, and no Jew would minister to a gentile. That is until one Jew from Galilee named Jesus came along. Jesus died for everyone! Not just one ethnic group. **John 13:34-35** says "a new commandment I give to you, that you love one another; as I have loved you, that you also love one another. By this all will know that you are My disciples, if you have love for one another."

Notice he did not point out one ethnic group. He said "love one another as I have loved you." Then He points out that the "love one another" part will let everyone know that you are one of His disciples. Can you honestly say that your actions toward another ethnic group show the love of Christ?

How many churches out there actually welcome people of other ethnicities with open arms? How many people have died and gone to Hell because some deacon or pastor of an all-White church or all-Black church, or any other church has kept someone out because of their skin color? One of the last things Christ said while He was still on Earth was "love your neighbor as yourself." I hope and pray that the reason you do not know your next-door neighbor's name, or why you don't eat lunch with certain co-workers, has nothing to do with the racial or ethnic group they happen to belong to.

I want to direct your attention to **Matthew 25: 1 – 46**. It says everything we do to the least of our brothers we do to Him! Everything you have ever done to someone else (judging, ignoring, making fun, passing over for a promotion, etc.) you are doing to Christ. How many of us have called Jesus a racial slur? Maybe we have made fun of Christ for the way He wears His clothes. Or maybe we have made fun of Him for the food He likes to eat.

I know you might be thinking, *I would never use a racial slur towards Jesus! Or make fun of Him for the way He wears his clothes, or the food that He eats.* But, according to Christ, if you have done anything of that nature to anyone you have done the same to Him. **Acts 10:34**, **Romans 2:11**, and **Ephesians 6:9** are just a few of the verses to start with if you are looking for Biblical guidance related to treating people the way a Christian is supposed to.

James 2 deals with interracial marriage. Whether it is all of Solomon's 300 wives or his father David's eight (that we know of), or Jacob's wives from various tribes and ethnicities, interracial marriage appears multiple times throughout the Bible. As a society we tend to put our own spin on what the Bible says based on our own preconceived ideas, or our own prejudices.

The one example I would like to concentrate on is in the book of **Numbers 12:1 – 10**. It has to do with Moses. He was a Hebrew raised as an Egyptian prince who killed a couple of guys then ran into the desert and stayed for 40 years. Then he returned and led the enslaved Hebrews out of Egypt.

Did you know that he married a Cushite woman? That was not looked on very well because she was (1) not a Jew and (2) was of a different ethnic background. She wasn't the same color as everyone else. That upset everyone, including Moses' brother and sister, Aaron and Miriam. Moses, the leader of God's people, was going to marry someone of a different ethnic background and Miriam and Aaron had begun to talk about Moses because of his Cushite wife (as some of us gossip about other people's lives).

"Has the Lord spoken only to Moses?" they asked. "Hasn't he also spoken through us?"

The Lord heard this and said to Moses, Aaron and Miriam, "Come out of the tent of meeting, all three of you."

So, all three of them went out. Then the Lord came down in a pillar of cloud and stood at the entrance of the tent and summoned Aaron and Miriam. When the two stepped forward, He said, "Listen to my words: when there is a prophet among you, I the Lord reveal Myself to them in visions; I speak to them in dreams. But this is not true of My servant Moses; he is faithful in My entire house. With him I speak face to face, clearly and not in riddles; He sees the form of the Lord, why then were you not afraid to speak against My servant Moses?" The anger of the Lord burned against them, and He left them. When the cloud had lifted from above the tent, Miriam's skin was leprous and became white as snow. Aaron turned towards her and saw that she had a defiling disease.

God punished Miriam with a defiling disease because she made fun of Moses for marrying a woman of a different ethnic background. That should tell you all you really need to know about interracial marriage, shouldn't it? God punished someone for making fun of an interracial couple.

Where do you stand on race as a Christian? Are you treating those of a different ethnic background fairly? Are you doing what Christ told you to do? Are you 'loving your neighbor as yourself' when it comes to race?

With all the things in this world that are wrong, how do we justify using a color to discern what kind of person someone is? In all my years on Earth the only thing I have seen that should be separated by color is laundry.

Romans 2:11 reads, "For there is no partiality with God." If God shows no partiality, why should we? If we can't be impartial, if we can't treat our neighbors as we treat ourselves, should we even be calling ourselves Christians?

Drinking Alcohol

Some Christians think less of people who consume alcohol, as though this is some unholy act. Although consuming alcohol is not forbidden in the Bible, it does give some very wise limits on it. For example, in the book of **Ephesians5:18**, "Do not get drunk on wine, which leads to debauchery" and in **Proverbs 20:1**, "Wine is a mocker and beer is a brawler; whoever is led astray by them is not wise."

Don't get me wrong, the slope from enjoying a glass of wine or a beer on the weekends or at dinner over to falling down drunk is a slippery one; which is why the Bible is crystal clear on why believers should not drink in excess. But for the believer, I think the best litmus test for this topic can be found in **Corinthians 10:31**, "So whether you eat or drink or whatever you do, do it all for the glory of God." If the activity you are engaging in doesn't do that, or you can't drink in moderation, then you should not be doing it at all. But if you can have a glass of wine or a drink at dinner and not get drunk, there is nothing biblically that says you can't. Not socializing with, befriending, or helping someone because they consume alcohol has everything to do with your judgement and nothing at all to do with the Bible. In case you forgot, we were commanded by Christ to drink wine (not orange juice, not spring water, not coffee, not tea) at communion.

Gossip

What is the most evil part of the body? The tongue! That thing gets all of us in more trouble than anything else we humans possess. We as Christians are constantly allowing that tiny part of our body to cause us problems. Gossiping is just another way we fail to show love to our neighbors.

The tongue has not only been the downfall of man, but also the angels. It was what got the Devil thrown out of Heaven. The Bible tells us that he had said in his heart that he would see his throne above God's. For humans, the story of Adam and Eve shows how a tongue can get us in a fix. After Adam ate the fruit that was presented to him by his wife, Eve, instead of taking responsibility for his disobedience, he very quickly pointed out that it was the woman God made him who had given him the fruit. Adam, with his tongue, not only blamed Eve but blamed the Almighty Himself for his own actions! How many of us has done that? Blamed someone else or even God for our own behavior?

So, what is it that compels us to continually say things that we should not be saying? Well, unfortunately there is a very simple answer to that. The tongue is difficult to manage.

Here is a list of verses that discuss how powerful the tongue is when it comes to sinning.

Proverbs 18:21: "Death and Life are in the power of the tongue, those that love it shall it eat its fruit."

This verse is telling us that those of us who love to gossip or use our words to break down other people, will eat the fruit of our words. In other words, you reap what you sow.

1 Peter 3:10: "For him that love life, and see good days, let him refrain his tongue from evil, and let his lips speak no guile."

In this verse we are being told that if we love life, we should not speak any evil.

Matthew 12:36-37: "But I say unto you, that every idle word that men shall speak, they shall give an account thereof in the Day of Judgment."

Read: Everything that we say that is evil or mean towards another person we will have to give an answer for.

How many things are you going to have to account for that you have said? I know I will have to give an account for a lot, like most people. Especially a lot of the things I said as a young man in my late teens and early twenties. I was not only a horrible man but a horrible person as well. But thankfully the Bible does say we can "tame" our tongue. Our tongue is being sinful when we do any of the following:

Proverbs 14:17: speak in anger.

Proverbs 18:13: speak when you don't have all the facts.

Proverbs 17:6: speak when you haven't verified a story.

1 Corinthians 8: 11: speak knowing your words will offend a weaker brother.

Peter 2: 21-23: speak when your words will be a poor reflection of the Lord or your family.

Proverbs 14:9: speak when you are tempted to joke about sin.

Proverbs 8:8: speak when you would be ashamed of your words later.

Ecclesiastes 5:2: speak when you are tempted to make light of holy things.

Proverbs 17:27: speak if your words will convey the wrong impression.

Proverbs 14:10: speak when the subject is none of your business.

Proverbs 4:24: speak when you are about to tell an outright lie.

Proverbs 16:27: speak if your words will hurt someone's reputation.

Proverbs 25:28: speak if you can't speak without yelling or your words will ruin a friendship.

James 3:9: speak when you are feeling critical.

Proverbs 13:1: speak when you should be listening.

Proverbs 18:21: speak if you may have to eat your words later.

Proverbs 19:13: speak when you have said something more than once.

Proverbs 24:24: speak when you are about to flatter a wicked person.

Proverbs 14:23: speak when you are supposed to be working instead.

And a final tidbit of wisdom from the Bible on this topic:

Proverbs 21:23: "whosoever keeps his tongue, keeps his soul from trouble!"

Though I saved you some time with my paraphrasing, I do encourage you to go read those passages for yourself so you can get the message directly from the text instead of having it filtered through me. As you read, ask yourself, "How I am doing when it comes to managing my tongue?"

Two of the issues that I see causing the most problems for people are (1) speaking when you don't have all the facts (i.e., gossip) and (2) speaking when you should be listening. If we could learn to ask more questions before we start speculating on an event or making things up about people, we could save a lot of friendships, respect our own reputations, and behave like true disciples of God.

If we could learn to listen more and talk less, we could avoid miscommunications, help the people around us feel listened to and respected, and keep ourselves from jumping to conclusions without hearing all the information. This helps us be more helpful to those around us by being a compassionate person who truly listens and doesn't just sit quietly, waiting to get our two cents in on the issue. Being a better listener helps us be a better friend, spouse, co-worker, parent, child, and overall human being because we are treating our neighbors with the respect and compassion they deserve.

All through this book I have been talking about the hypocrisy of the modern Christians. The tongue is where the rubber meets the road. We are human. It is in our very nature to attack things we do not like or understand.

So, if hypocrisy starts with the tongue, how do we control it? It's difficult. We are a sinful bunch after all. **James 1:26** says that if anyone thinks he is religious and does not bridle his tongue but deceives his heart, this person's religion is worthless.

How many "super-religious" people do you know who can't control their tongue? Are you that way? If so, you are making your religion useless by the words you speak.

Religion and our differences over it have caused war, famine, and murder since Cain and Abel. Let's stop trying to be "holy rollers" and just focus on loving people. A single verse, if heeded, could make us all better people, and it's from **Exodus 14:14**: "The Lord will fight for you; you only must remain silent."

We all know that remaining silent and sitting still is not easy. This is evident in the way hatred and judgement are spouted from the modern Christian's mouth, even from the pulpit. We say we want to save the sinner, but we stand at the door every Sunday and tell them how evil they are or that they are not welcome because of their looks, financial status, alternate lifestyle, etc. So, how are we supposed to tell them about or show them the love of Christ if we won't even let them in the door? Remember that religion is manmade, while love is God-made.

Jesus never went to the temple to find the lost, He went where they were. He ate with tax collectors and prostitutes. Have you followed in His footsteps in this way? Why not? How will you ever get the lost to Christ if you never interact with them?

How can you call yourself a believer or a follower of Christ if you are not doing the work He charged us with? The truth is most of us can't say that we are true followers of Christ. Yes, we go to church on Sunday, we might even put some money in the collection plate, but any random person can do those things. What makes you different from the average person? What makes you an obvious follower of the teachings of Christ and the word of God?

I want to end this chapter with some quotes about minding your tongue, as well as some quotes from famous neighbor-lovers, and a poem by James Patrick Kinney that perfectly complements this section. Use these as prompts to consider your own level of devotion to God and how you're using (or not using) any and all parts of yourself to love—or hate—your neighbor.

"Give thy thoughts no tongue."

—William Shakespeare

"All parts of the human body get tired eventually-except the tongue."

—Konrad Adenaure

"The tongue is the only thing that gets sharper with use."
—Washington Irving

"A gentle answer turns away wrath, but a harsh word stirs up anger."
—Solomon

"Give me a ready hand rather than the ready tongue."
—Cesare Pavese

"A person's tongue can give you the taste of his heart"
—Ibn Qayum Al-Jawziyya

"Better to slip foot than tongue."
—Benjamin Franklin

"No one is born hating another person because of the color of his skin, or his background, or his religion. People must learn to hate, and if they can learn to hate, they can be taught to love, for love comes more naturally to the human heart that its opposite."
—Nelson Mandela, *Long Walk to Freedom*

"Hating people because of their color is just wrong and it doesn't matter what color does the hating it is just plain wrong."
—Muhammad Ali

"If we cannot end our differences, at least we can help make the world safe for diversity."

—John F. Kennedy

"Darkness cannot drive out darkness, only light can do that. Hate cannot drive out hate. Only love can do that."

—Dr. Martin Luther King, Jr.

"If you want see the measure of a man, watch how he treats his inferiors, not his equals."

—J.K. Rowling

The Cold Within
By James Patrick Kinney

Six humans trapped by happenstance
In bleak and bitter cold.
Each one possessed a stick of wood
Or so the story's told.

Their dying fire in need of logs,
The first one held hers back
For, of the faces around the fire
She noticed one was black.

The next man looking 'cross the way
Saw one not of his church
And could not bring himself to give
The first his stick of birch.

The third one sat in tattered clothes.
He gave his coat a hitch.
Why should his log be put to use
To warm the idle rich?

The rich man just sat back and thought
Of the wealth he had in store,
And how to keep what he had earned
From the lazy, shiftless poor.

The black man's face bespoke revenge
As the first passed from his sight
For all he saw in his stock of wood
Was a chance to spite the white.

The last man of this forlorn group
Did nought except for gain
Giving only to those who gave
Was how he played the game.

Their logs held tight in death's still hands
Was proof of human sin.
They did not die from the cold without
The died from the cold within.

Chapter Summary

What traditions are you holding on to that may keep you from loving people?

_____

_____

_____

_____

_____

Do traditions or habits cause you to hate? Do you think following traditions will get you to Heaven?

_____

_____

_____

_____

_____

Do you use your tongue to spout hate or love? How?

_____

_____

_____

_____

_____

_____

_____

_____

_____

_____

How many people do you think you've hurt with your tongue?
In what ways? How can you do better with this in the future?

_____
_____
_____
_____
_____

How can your tongue turn people away from knowing God?

_____
_____
_____
_____
_____

When was the last time you interacted with someone of a
different race? Did you do anything to show them love?

_____
_____
_____
_____
_____
_____
_____
_____
_____
_____

Have you ever told a racist joke? Have you ever laughed at a racist joke that was told? Have you ever asked someone not to tell a joke because it was racist?

_____

_____

_____

_____

_____

Do you tend to hang out only with people of your race and ethnic background? Why is this? Are you comfortable with considering widening your social circle?

_____

_____

_____

_____

_____

Have you avoided spending time with someone or talking to someone because of the food they eat, music they listen to, way they dress, or any other superficial issue?

_____

_____

_____

_____

_____

_____

_____

_____

_____

Do you choose books, television shows, or movies based on how similar the main character is to you? When is the last time you read a book, watched a television show, or saw a movie in which the main character was of a different race, gender, sexual orientation, nationality, or religious affiliation than your own?

_____
_____
_____
_____
_____

_____
_____
_____
_____
_____

Chapter 4
Making Disciples

Go and make disciples.

I can hear you now thinking, *That's not my job! That's the church's job.* I have news for you—you **are** the church!

The commandment to go and make disciples was given to all of us, not just pastors. But you might understandably be wondering how to get started or how to even define a disciple. To help you, I will now outline the answers to these and similar questions related to making disciples.

The first step is always to work on yourself. Put a heartfelt effort into being the best Christian you can so you can serve as a strong, spiritually attractive example for all the people around you, not just your church friends.

Once you believe that your spiritual strength is higher and you are consistently following the commandments to love God with all your heart and mind and to love your neighbors, you're ready to start going out into the world and making disciples. This may seem difficult or even frightening, but it's doable and necessary for the health of your church and your own spirit. Satan, of course, wants you to only sit in church and still consider yourself a good Christian. Because if you do that, you're not going out into the world and inviting others to join in worshipping God. Satan already has to worry about trying to break your faith in God, he doesn't want to have to worry about the number of Christians in the world growing because each believer is going out into the world and bringing back more lost souls.

Follower, Disciple, or Dummy?

People ask me all the time what religion I follow. I tell them that I don't follow a religion, I follow, and am a disciple of, Jesus Christ. Most people who consider themselves Christians fall into three main categories—follower, disciple, or dummy.

Followers have a dictionary definition of "an adherent or devotee of a particular person, cause, or activity." You likely consider yourself a follower of Jesus Christ. I like to refine the characteristics of a follower of Jesus Christ a little further for clarity. Followers of Jesus Christ:

- Go to church on Sundays.
- Listen to the message delivered by the preacher.
- Try to be a good person.
- Volunteer at church by leading the choir or teaching Sunday school.
- Host a Bible study or other church activity.

While there's nothing wrong with being a follower of Christ, and you are doing a portion of what Jesus commanded, you're not fully realizing your role. Worship doesn't truly happen in the church. Worship takes place when we go feed the hungry, find shelter for the homeless, and take care of the sick—none of which can be done very well from a pew.

A disciple is a student of a teacher, leader, or philosopher. Like an apprentice, their role is to carry out their leader's teachings and directives. A follower's faith is internally felt, while a disciple's faith is externally shown. Most of us, if we analyzed our actions, would find that we behave in ways that show our value of greed, pride, vanity, and gluttony (I need a bigger paycheck, more expensive house, newer car, etc.). In other words, we often act like disciples of Satan rather than worshippers of God.

You can't go out and make disciples if you are not one yourself. And you should not consider yourself a disciple if you are any of the following:

- Racist
- Homophobic
- Prideful
- Vain
- Judgmental
- Hypocritical
- A gossip

A true disciple is:

- Loving
- A servant of others
- Loving
- A servant of others
- Loving
- A servant of others

We say "hate the sin, not the sinner," but we don't go out to get the sinners and bring them to God. You are not a disciple if you are not doing this.

Dummies are just what they sound like: something designed to resemble and serve as a substitute for the real or usual thing; a counterfeit or sham. Unfortunately, the term 'dummy' includes a huge chunk of people who call themselves Christians. Dummies:

- Go to church each Sunday to be seen in their new clothes or car and gossip about the rest of the congregation (often won't go to church if hair, nails, clothes, and other superficial settings aren't the way they like).
- Complain about everything from the musical selections during service to how hot or cold the sanctuary is that day.
- Listen to the message just enough so that they can throw the highlights in someone else's face later on (because none of the sermon applies to them—EVER).
- Gossip about others in the congregation—the dress Suzy has on, the teenage girl that's pregnant, the business owner who just filed bankruptcy, etc.

As a group, we Christians really need to get this situation in hand. We are leaving our children a legacy of hate, judgment, and criticism. There isn't a single passage in the Bible that commands that we hate anyone else. Remembering and incorporating this truth into our everyday lives is critical to becoming our best Christian selves.

Meeting the Lost Where They Are

"The Great Commission says to make disciples, not get followers. There is a difference."

—Miguel Nunez

"You have one business on earth, to save souls."
—John Wesley

"The Gospel is only Good News if it gets there in time."
—Carl F.H. Henry

"If a commission by an earthly king is considered an honor, how can a commission by a heavenly king be considered a sacrifice?"
—David Livingston

I hope that you understand what The Great Commission is and why it is so important to the movement of the kingdom of God. We all must remember that we only have three simple rules to follow, and if we do follow those rules there will be no limit as to the souls we can bring to Christ. But chaperoning a church youth event is not enough. This is like trying to save people from a burning building without leaving the fire station.

What is a Pastor?

What is a pastor supposed to do? What's they're actual job? Can a woman lead a church?

The Latin word 'pastor' means "shepherd." But when it comes to leading a congregation of people attempting to follow God's will, what does that look like?

Some of the essential knowledge and skills a pastor should have include:

- Strong character.

- Impartiality.
- Good public speaking skills.
- Compassion for others.
- Ability to communicate with clarity.

If you read this list and didn't see your current pastor on it, I encourage you to find another "shepherd." But if you think that your current pastor has all of these qualities, it sounds like you might be in good hands. In **Timothy 4:2** it states pastors should: "preach the word; be prepared in season and out of season; correct, rebuke, and encourage with great patience and careful instruction."

This verse lets us know that preaching the word is important. But many pastors seem to be too busy arguing over which translation of the Bible to use, or what kind of music plays in the church, or how much money they *didn't* see in the collection plate this week to focus on God. Preaching is only a small piece of what a pastor must do, and yet it is a crucial component.

Being prepared in and out of season means being so steeped in their faith and their God that someone asking them a simple question is no problem at all, especially a question about Jesus, God, or the Bible. I can't tell you how many times I've heard a pastor get asked a question and his answer be that he doesn't know, followed by an (often broken) promise to "get back to" the person about an answer. That doesn't seem prepared to me. Especially when that's a pastor's response more often than not.

When it comes to correcting, rebuking, and encouraging, many pastors have the first two down to a science. They can correct and rebuke with the best of them, especially if it comes to someone saying or doing something that doesn't align with *the pastor's* line of thought (not necessarily the Bible's). Oddly, encouragement is often lacking in pastors. They are ready and willing to be encouraging when someone has passed away. They don't mind encouraging grieving widows or children. But when it comes to encouraging people to go out and use God's love to touch the lives of others, or encouraging people to try to make amends for things they've done wrong, or encouraging people to finish trade school or get a university degree, they're seldom seen doing so. This is not to say that when you're suffering you don't need encouragement, but there are things that pastors should be encouraging you to do on a daily basis beyond putting your faith in God's plan for someone's eternal rest.

Confidence in Leadership

Hebrews 13:17 states, "Obey those who rule over you, and be submissive, for they watch out you're your souls, as those who must give account. Let them do so with joy and not with grief, for that would be unprofitable for you." This passage denotes that pastors are not the "end all be all" authority in the church. They were called on by God, just like leaders and teachers of other kinds who do God's work. You know this because the "must give account" to the being who has authority over all of us: God. They will have to testify about how they helped and watched over you. And your job is to obey and make their work a joy, and not a burden. It wouldn't benefit you to have someone who is supposed to be helping guide you be overwhelmed, disrespected, belittled, or abused. Then they can't do all that they can in order to help you.

One of the major problems I see with pastors today is that being a pastor has become attempt to get a paycheck as opposed to being a calling like it should be. A pastor should not be as concerned about his career goals as he is about growing God's Kingdom. **James 3:1** tells us, "My brethren, let now many of you become teachers, knowing that we shall receive a stricter judgment." So any pastors who are reading this, I hope you understand that you are being held to a higher standard than the average worshipper, and God will not be satisfied with someone just looking for a check.

Female Pastors

I have heard all sorts of reasons for and against the idea of a woman being a pastor. Many of the people I know who are opposed to the idea of a woman preaching point to the apostle Paul. Namely, Timothy 2:12, when *Paul* (not God, not Jesus) stated, "And I do not permit a woman to teach or to have authority over a man, but to be in silence." This means that Paul was giving his opinion on the matter. And let's not forget that Paul was a rabbi (not a priest or pastor) during a time when women were socially and legally considered property.

And yet, Paul did speak highly of Phoebe and a few other women. And there were many women who surrounded the ministry of Christ as well as donated financially to the ministry. Like even mentions a few by name, Mary Magdalene being the most prominent.

I'll lay out my own thoughts here. I believe that women can preach. Women were present at the Pentecost and went out and preached. Jesus said go and tell the good news, and He said that to every believer, not just men. However, I do not believe that women should be the lead pastors in a church.

Getting Fed

Hopefully, you go to church to get spiritually fed and that is what the pastor does for you. I'll not again that no apostles spoke in many churches. Jesus said go into the world, not a building. He said there is no temple in Heaven. And the ones we have here on Earth shouldn't exist if all they're going to do is divide us or make us unite under a set of silly, non-biblical traditions.

Stopping at the Cross

Just as you weren't born a strong Christian, neither will the people who do finally give their lives over to God become strong without support. Though I haven't run into very many churches who engage in outreach to bring the lost to God, of those who do, very rarely is there a plan in place for ongoing training for these newly-saved souls. They might go as far as to baptize someone, and then they're on their own as a new worshipper.

My advice is not to stop at the cross. When a newcomer to your congregation, or just a new person you're meeting in your every day life, hands themselves over the God, disciple-making starts with becoming a spiritual mentor for them. When people feel connected to something, they're more likely to stick with it. You have it in your power to be the connection that keeps someone in the faith and frequenting your house of worship. Prepare them for what we are told to do by Jesus. Help them know and understand the Great Commission and the three commandments outlined in this book. This is a way to show God's love so that they can fill themselves with it and then go give some to others.

In the last chapter, we'll go over some things you can do that will put all three of the commandments we've discussed into action.

"Religion is a very scary thing, because a pastor is in a position of power. And if you use that power badly, you ruin people's lives, and you will ruin your own life."

—Eugene H. Peterson.

"We don't forget that we are Christians. We forget that we are human, and that one oversight alone can debilitate the potential of our future."

—Wayne Corderio

"Great leaders are teachable leaders."

—Gary Rohrmayer

'We are all faced with a series of great opportunities brilliantly disguised as impossible situations."

—Chuck Swindoll

Chapter Summary

Do you think you are a follower, disciple, or dummy? Why do you think this about yourself?

_____

_____

_____

_____

_____

What do you do on a regular basis that helps to grow God's kingdom? If you can't think of anything, what do you think has been keeping you from helping grow God's kingdom (guidance, knowledge, time, money, etc.)?

_____

_____

_____

_____

_____

_____

_____

_____

_____

_____

_____

_____

_____

_____

What are your church's outreach programs? Do they help people outside of the congregation or are they for church members only?

_____

_____

_____

_____

_____

Has your pastor been called or does it seem like they're just in their position for a salary or prestige? What have you heard or seen them do or say that helped you form your opinion of them?

_____

_____

_____

_____

_____

_____

_____

_____

Does it seem like your pastor is actually preaching the word of God or more like they're pushing a political agenda? Does your pastor preach love and forgiveness or hate and judgement?

_____

_____

_____

Chapter 5
Next Steps

Worshipping God with all our minds and souls, loving our neighbors, and going out to make disciples are three intense tasks. But they are necessary to grow the kingdom of God and they are necessary to become Christians who have reached are full potentials as worshippers of God. In this chapter, I offer you options for ways you can adhere to the three commandments discussed in this book. If you think of more, feel free to do those as well!

Worshipping God

If you want to worship God, it helps to study the Bible. If you're a fellow Southerner, you've probably heard all your life that the "one true" Bible is the King James version (KJV). As the name implies, it's helpful to remember that this is a *single version* of the Bible. I would argue it is the most political version around. The Bible was originally written in Hebrew and Greek, not English. The English version did not come around until the late 1300s, translated by John Wycliffe and furthered by William Tyndale in the 1500s. The KJV wasn't translated until 100 years after that, based on the language and customs of that time. But as we gather more knowledge about antiquated cultures and language, we're better able to understand what was meant by each word used in the Bible, and we learn more about the Bible and Christianity as a whole.

But, at the end of the day, King James was an Atheist. So stating that his version of the Bible is the one true version sounds strange to me and it's ironic that it has come to have such a hold over our lives and beliefs as Christians. The KJV was translated under his direct orders, so anything he wanted added, subtracted, or re-worded would be altered as he saw fit. That's not to necessarily say that his version is a "bad" one. But it is a politically, not spiritually, motivated one. While I do believe that there is only one true Bible, I think it would be a mistake to believe that there is only one valid English translation. We must have great respect for the text and we do need to study the word of God with a similar as our current scholars continually study the ancient text.

Before you begin studying your next section of the Bible, I encourage you to pray to God and ask Him to show you what you need to see. If you do that, I promise it will not matter what English translation you have, you will get what was intended by Him.

Worship God by:
- Praying for patience and compassion to pass along to all the humans the God created (even the ones that annoy, frustrate, sadden, or scare you sometimes).
- Praying for patience and compassion for yourself as you strive to grow as a human and as a Christian (this isn't easy and you should avoid getting down on yourself about mistakes).
- Loving your fellow human beings (ALL OF THEM!).
- Attracting others to God through your own honesty, goodness, and open-hearted demeanor (make people want to peace of mind, confidence, and spiritual comfort you enjoy because of your relationship with God).
- Focusing on why *you* already love God, not why someone else should start.

Loving Your Neighbors

Love your neighbors by:

- Not judging or criticizing people because they act, speak, behave, look, or live differently than you. This can take a lot of time and effort (after all, you didn't learn to be judgmental overnight!), so be patient with yourself.
- Going to places you wouldn't normally go in order to help others (soup kitchens, poverty-stricken neighborhoods, storm-devastated cities, etc.). This will help you gain compassion for people regardless of how similar they are to you or how different they are from you.
- Get to know your physical neighbors. The people next door, behind you, across the street, even at the end of the cul-de-sac. Do you know their names or where they're from? Consider inviting them over for dinner, a cookout, or a watch party. Remember that this is about getting to know them so that you can show them love and respect. **This is not a conversion attempt!** However, if they have specific questions about how you worship, be open and honest with them about your beliefs.
- Be thoughtful. Consider people's possible needs and ask if you can be of assistance. If an elderly co-worker has trouble with stairs, help them as you come to work and leave work together. If a neighbor is a single parent, offer to run errands like shopping or mowing the lawn to help give them a few extra minutes each

week to recharge or spend more quality (non-errand) time with their kids.

- Help people in the service industry. Give generous tips to restaurant servers, hotel porters, or delivery drivers.
- Invest in your fellow humans. Give to Kickstarters and GoFundMe pages. Offer to buy a new suit for someone who is job hunting, or a new car for someone who is forced to drive one that's on its last legs. If you aren't blessed enough financially to do things like this, consider what you can do with your time. Can you run a few social media profiles for an entrepreneur while they go drum up business? Could you teach, tutor, mentor, or otherwise guide people who may have lots of talent, but little business or financial savvy?

Go and Make Disciples

Go out into the world and draw as many people as you can into the love and grace of God.

Go and make disciples by:

- Raising your children (or other young family members such as nephews and nieces) to be loving and kind through their Christian faith. Don't force or rope them into following manmade traditions so that they can go through the motions of being a "dummy" Christian. Show them how to go out and change the world in the name of God's love.
- Following up with and supporting people who have recently given their mind, heart, and soul to our Lord. Don't just congratulate them for "joining the club" and then leave them all alone.

- Getting out of the pew and out into the real world.
  Meeting people where they are is critical for getting
  them to understand the love that God has for us all—
  no matter what we've been through; no matter what
  sins we've committed. Consider the kinds of people
  who you think could benefit most from God's love—
  orphans, people living with drug addiction or mental
  illness, poor people having to live with multiple
  families in a single apartment, homeless veterans
  suffering from PTSD—and go find them where they
  are. Don't wait for them to wander into your church.

In Conclusion

Throughout this short book, I have written about a lot
of the things we as Christians do that give us a bad name. We
are told we must live in this evil world, but we do not have to
be like it. Our actions as Christians have done nothing but turn
today's youth away from God. Even more sadly, our narrow-
minded dogmatic points of view have kept us from doing what
we all should be doing: reaching the lost!

Fixing this issue means letting go of our judgmental
ways. Not one time in the Bible do you see Christ reserving his
time and attention for the "church crowd." He was off sharing
a meal with a poor person or having conversations with
sexual deviants and other rejects of society. The few times He
even set foot in a 'religious' home or came across a 'religious'
crowd, He consistently admonished them for treating people
poorly when they should be loving them.

Being a Christian, I'm sure you already know most of
these things from having read them in the Bible or heard
about them during a sermon. But the key ingredient to
fulfilling our purposes as Christians and helping to grow the

kingdom of God is that we must act on what we know and *show* it to the non-Christians among us, not just speak about it.

Remember to pray and ask God to show you what you need to see as you study His word and go out to do work in His name. We all need to learn to love again or we will soon be just as evil as the world makes us out to be.

May the peace of our Lord Jesus Christ be with you all. Amen.

Chapter Summary

Which of the tips in this chapter did you try out for yourself (eating dinner with a neighbor, helping clean up after a storm hits, etc.)? What was it like? Would you do it again?

_____

_____

_____

_____

_____

_____

Go back to the beginning of the book and look at some of your answers to the chapter summary questions. Are there any you would change after reading the entire book? Why or why not?

_____

_____

_____

_____

_____

Write down one thing you can do this week that will show love to someone else.

_____

_____

_____

_____

_____

Go and research a particular activity or group you could volunteer with in order to help show God's love to others. Write the information down here. How do you think you will increase your spiritual health by getting involved with this event / organization?

_____
_____
_____
_____
_____

Write down the names of some people in your life you think you can be of service to and *how* you might be of service to them. Don't forget to contact each one and let them know what you're willing to do for them if they need it!

_____
_____
_____
_____
_____
_____
_____
_____
_____

Acknowledgements

I would like to thank God for sending His son, Jesus, to die for me. As well as for the courage, strength, and knowledge to finish this project. It is only through His gifts that I can do this.

Thank you, Lord, for sending me out of the wasteland!

Dear Reader:

I would like to take the time to thank you for giving my book a chance. Although brief, I believe it conveys the message that was in my heart when I wrote it. I want to clarify that what you've just read was not mean to be an attack on the church or its teachings. I simply want for all of us who call ourselves followers of Christ to take an honest look in the mirror. The Christian reputation is being dragged through the mud and unfortunately it is we Christians who put ourselves in that position every day based on the way we behave. I want this book to be a wakeup call to us all. Before we can point the finger at anyone for making the word "Christian" a laughable thing, we must first point a finger at ourselves.

I truly believe I was led to write this to do just that. We must, as disciples of Christ, get back to His teachings and lead the world in love and forgiveness. We can't do that if we are constantly spouting hatred of other races, alternative lifestyles, or each other based on useless bits of traditions we made up as we went along.

Jesus told us to love, not to hate. We do not have to agree with the world or what the people in it do. But we do have to love.

Thank you,
Dr. Michael C. Burkhalter

Special Thanks

First, I would like to thank my parents, P.P. Carl "Buck" Burkhalter & Jeanette C. Burkhalter, because without you two I would not know or understand what true love is.

Sylvia Diane "Poochie" Fuller for showing me that it does not matter what life gives you, it is how you handle it that counts.

My children (Ashlee, Oceana, and Caylee) for giving me the joy of being a father and the proof that God has a sense of humor.

My grandchildren Gage, Elliot, Rezmay, Nathan, J.P., and Penny for reminding me that the youth are the future and that we must strive to teach you the right path.

Trevor Swaney for taking care of my oldest daughter and my grandkids and for your service to our country.

Leeann Rutz for all the great meals you fed me and for showing me how to love friends as much as family.

Donna Kay Ross for all the encouragement since we lost Leeann. Poochie, Mom, Dad and Ronald would not have made it through that without you.

Ronald C. Burkhalter for every lesson about cars I could ever want to hear, and the boldness to say what needs to be said even if it hurts.

James Carey for treating me as a son instead of a nephew, and of course, for teaching me about love and life, as well as how to cheer for the two best football teams on Earth—the Clemson Tigers and the Washington Redskins.

Kenny E. Lyda for helping me understand what being a brother means and for showing me that even a good person can cheer for the wrong sports teams.

Chris J. Fuller for showing me that even the little brother can teach you some valuable lessons; even if you are a Tennessee fan.

Aaron Davis for being a friend and a fellow disciple of Christ that has shown me that actions speak way louder than words ever can.

Eddie Cox for being my pastor and for showing me the difference between a follower of Christ and a disciple of Christ.

Jeff Mousa for all those conversations we have had and all the challenges you have given me. You truly inspire me to challenge my own thinking and dig deeper into the word.

Alicia Haack for being a friend and always keeping me on my toes.

Barry L. Reese for being there when I was going through the most difficult time in my life, and for all the life lessons I learned under you as a teacher and band director. But most of all for the knowledge and love you showed to every student you ever taught and making sure we all were cared for and taken care of.

Tessa Haack for asking the tough questions and the strength in God that you have.

Diane Buice for reminding me why I teach what I do.

Jesse Haack:

I am sure a simple thank you would be enough for you. But you deserve a little more than that. Thank you for being my friend and student all these years. Thank you for the conversations, tough questions, and incredible answers that really shouldn't come out of someone your age. I know that you will go on to do great things before you are called home. My life has truly improved since we first met. Thank you.

Your friend,
Michael

Lea,

Words cannot truly express how I feel about you. Through all the ups and downs in my life over the past year, you have been there. Not always in the greatest way, but in *your* way. That's what I fell in love with. Thank you for pushing me to finish this project and for encouraging me to do more. I cannot wait for you to be my wife and I will do everything that I can to improve the love I have for you, Kelly, and Landon. I know we have had great times and horrible times over the past year, but I am happy for all the times both good and bad. They show we can make it through any storm if we trust in God and each other. So please do not let go of my hand as we walk through life together.

I love you,
Michael

Thank you for reading
***Cast the First Stone* by Michael Burkhalter!**

To learn more about Michael Burkhalter, please visit his site at DocMikesBlog.wordpress.com.

Made in the USA
Monee, IL
15 July 2023

39305462R00046